True HORSE Stories

Brigadier

GENTLE HERO

BY JUDY ANDREKSON

Illustrations by David Parkins

Tundra Books

Published in Canada by Tundra Books,
75 Sherbourne Street, Toronto, Ontario M5A 2P9

Published in the United States by Tundra Books of Northern New York,
P.O. Box 1030, Plattsburgh, New York 12901

Library of Congress Control Number: 2008902999

Library and Archives Canada Cataloguing in Publication

Andrekson, Judy
Brigadier : gentle hero / Judy Andrekson ; illustrated by David Parkins.
(True horse stories)

ISBN 978-0-88776-904-7

1. Brigadier (Horse) – Juvenile literature. 2. Police horses – Ontario –
Toronto – Biography – Juvenile literature. 3. Animal heroes – Biography –
Juvenile literature. I. Parkins, David II. Title. III. Series.

HV7957.A54 2009   J636.1'08860929   C2008-902091-X

We acknowledge the financial support of the Government of Canada through the
Book Publishing Industry Development Program (BPIDP) and that of the
Government of Ontario through the Ontario Media Development Corporation's
Ontario Book Initiative. We further acknowledge the support of the Canada
Council for the Arts and the Ontario Arts Council for our publishing program.

Design: Terri Nimmo

ONTARIO ARTS COUNCIL
CONSEIL DES ARTS DE L'ONTARIO

Printed and bound in Canada

This book is printed on acid-free paper that is 100% recycled,
ancient-forest friendly (100% post-consumer recycled).

1 2 3 4 5 6   14 13 12 11 10 09

To Kate, the best 'right hand woman'
a mom could ever hope for.
I love you, kiddo.

And for two very special women
in my life, Sally and Gran (Marg).

Acknowledgments

I would like to express my sincere thanks to the many special people who made the telling of this story possible. This story touched me, as a writer and as an animal lover, because of the caring and love that I continually encountered while interviewing the people who had been affected by Brigadier's short life. The connection between human and non-human life is so important, and I have rarely seen it in play as eloquently as it was here.

Thank you so much to Anne de Haas for first putting me on the path of the right person to get started, and for your beautiful photographs and the memories you shared with me. Your contributions to this book are immense and so appreciated. Gayle Ecker (University of Guelph), David Carson, and Vicki Montgomery, thanks to each of you for sharing and adding your voices to this story. Graham Acott, Kevin Bradfield, Ronald Gilbert, and Tim Crone – each of you were touched by this great horse, and each of you deeply moved me with your memories. Thank you so much. Ted Gallipeau – I never had the chance to speak with you in person, but the stories told to me about your time with Brigadier had me feeling as though I knew you well. Thank you for being a part of this. Finally, a special thanks to Staff Inspector William (Bill) Wardle, who supplied an endless amount of difficult information, CDs, books, contacts, and his own heart toward the creation of Brig's story. I am very grateful to you.

Thank you to all members of the Mounted and Police Dog Services who work daily with these special animals and understand, more than most, the horse/human bond I attempt to portray in all of my books.

Contents

Prologue

*T*here are times in this life when such tragic, senseless things happen that it's hard for us to fathom them. As humans, we are capable of goodness and nobility, and also cruelty and pain. This is our nature.

Sometimes, however, when we look under the surface of an event, we see much more than the tragedy. We see love and hope and a cause for change, and things start to make sense again.

Such is the story of Brigadier . . . at least, that is how the story affected me. When I first heard of him, I was struck by the sadness and sheer horror of the event that he had been involved in. As an animal lover, I experienced the anger and helplessness, followed by the feeling of outrage that comes when a senseless act of harm is committed against an innocent creature.

As I looked deeper, though, I found that the shocking act that brought Brigadier to the attention of the world was not at all what this horse was about. Brigadier's story is not one of tragedy and loss. It is a story of a life well lived, and of special relationships, in which a four-legged hero is no less than his two-legged partner. It is a story of courage, gentleness, humor, growth, and, of course, great love.

This is Brigadier's story. . . .

I

Gentle Giant

*I*ce crystals glittered in the crisp, January air as Graham Acott guided the truck and trailer off the main road and onto the long, narrow driveway leading to David Carson's farm. Despite the frigid weather,  the drive to Listowel had been a pleasant break from the city hustle and bustle of Toronto, Ontario. The scenery had become steadily more peaceful as he'd traveled west for the past ninety minutes. It had changed from the busy streets of downtown Toronto, to the sprawling suburb areas, to acreages, and finally to rolling farmland. Snow covered the land like a sparkling blanket and Graham felt the tension leaving his shoulders as the miles slipped by and he headed into horse country.

"Do you still think we're takin' the right horse back, Sarge? I liked that bay better."

Graham glanced at the officer sitting beside him and smiled. "I'm sure," he said in his usual laconic style. And he was sure.

After twenty-two years of riding, training, and assessing horses for the Mounted Unit of the Toronto Police Department, Graham Acott knew exactly what he was looking for, and he felt absolutely certain that he had found it in the horse they were going to pick up now.

Graham and his younger partner had been to David Carson's farm a few weeks earlier, looking for a possible remount (a young horse to replace an aging one), to add to their stable of twenty-seven other horses. David had been supplying animals to the Mounted Unit for many years, and knew just the type of horse they liked. He had presented three geldings for consideration, all very worthy young horses, but only one had stood out for Graham.

The horses had to be a certain type – big and sturdy with quiet temperaments, but with enough fire to withstand rigorous training and long work days. They needed to be over sixteen hands high, between three to five years old, and black, bay, or chestnut in color. Draft crosses, known as grade horses, were preferable, as it added size and bone and a steady mind to the mounts, and these were David's specialty.

David Carson was a farmer with a hand in many pots. He had several large sections of farmland – some for cattle, and some for the hundred or more head of horses he owned, bred, trained, leased, sold, and even raced. The main farm, where Graham and his partner were now, included a large stable and indoor training arena, an indoor, two-ring auction service for animals and machinery, as well as a tack shop. The buildings and surrounding area were impressively tidy and well kept. The whole place rang of professionalism.

One of the many special services David offered was a supply of nurse mares, or mares with milk available to nurse orphaned foals. Sometimes inexperienced mares will reject their newborns, or they may be too ill to raise their foal. Some even die. David's gentle draft mares were perfect for the job of foster dam, and his fee for this service often included having the nurse mare bred back to a lighter breed of stallion if there was one available on the farm where she was on loan.

Five years earlier, one of his gentlest Belgian mares had fostered a foal on a nearby thoroughbred farm where a lanky, fine-boned, fiery stallion stood at stud. The mare had been bred to this stallion before returning to David's farm, and the following spring, a colt had been born. He was a golden chestnut with four white stockings and a long, jagged blaze running the full length of his broad face.

This was the colt Graham had come to pick up on that chilly January afternoon. There was something special about this big gelding; a certain kindness in his dark eyes and a gentle expression that made Graham choose him over the more spectacular-looking bay colt his partner had fancied. From what David told him, the colt had been sweet-natured from the start.

The colt had been pasture born and raised, with no difficulties or incidents. His dam had been an attentive giant of a mother, experienced in raising both her own and other mares' foals, and with a disposition as gentle as any horse could have. He spent his early months roaming the large, open broodmare pasture of David's horse farm, never far from his safe and sturdy dam or the herd of other broodmares and their foals.

He loved to play, running and bucking and nipping at the other colts and fillies, but at a nicker from his dam, he was back at her side, nursing and resting under her watchful, gentle eye.

The colt was halter-broke during the autumn of his first year, when he was taken from his mother for weaning. He had been in contact with humans from the day of his birth and loved to be handled and rubbed and played with, as many foals do. However, the restricting sensation of the halter, added to the anxiety of being taken forever from the protective side of his dam, was enough to cause even the sweetest foal to throw a tantrum. His was mild compared to some.

He was named Danny Boy by the stable hands, and after a few days of pitiful whinnying and fence-pacing, he adjusted to life as a weanling. In his loneliness, he responded even more affectionately to the humans who were watching over him, rubbing his shaggy, baby head against them, seeking reassurance and companionship.

His friendliness ensured that he was one of the more sought-after colts during the humans' daily visits to the pasture, and so he was handled regularly in an unofficial sort of way. Except for the early halter training, he had very little formal handling or schooling of any kind until he turned two.

His first two years were spent growing and developing strong bones and muscles on the natural, rolling pastures of the farm. He was toughened by the seasonal weather conditions he bore without special protection, along with the dozens of other horses with whom he shared his space. He was not a pampered stable horse, and had developed no bad habits by the time he was old enough to begin formal training.

By the time he was a two year old, he was already close to sixteen hands, with the heavy bones and strong build of his dam, but with enough refinement from his thoroughbred sire to make him useful as a riding horse. He was impressive looking – a gleaming golden chestnut with a powerful, arched neck and big, round, solid feet. Always curious, his dark eyes watched everything that happened around him, and his innate gentleness gained him friends.

Danny Boy was moved to the main farm as a two year old, where he would be nearer the training facilities and the action of a busy, working farm and auction company. He was handled regularly now, groomed almost daily, and introduced to the farrier, who trimmed his hooves and later shod him.

He was started on lunge work – moving in circles on a long line around his trainer. He soon understood basic word commands such as walk, trot, canter, whoa, back, and reverse. He learned to pay attention to his handler and that this human/horse relationship was about more than treats and rubs in the pasture. He was getting ready to work, although most of his time was still spent at leisure in the fields.

Danny Boy was trained to harness and to the western saddle late in his third year, by which time he had reached his full height of sixteen point one hands (sixty-five inches) and a weight of almost fifteen hundred pounds. He was a big horse with a big, kind heart, and he took to his training without a fuss.

The colt impressed David. It didn't seem to matter what he asked of him, Danny Boy would try his best to figure it out. You just had to show him once or twice, and he got it. He quickly learned about the long-reins – David even drove him into town at times to "de-spook" him – and the saddle and bridle. The big horse seemed unconcerned when he first felt the weight of a human on his back, and he caught on to basic cues of hands, legs, and voice.

David decided that the gelding was a good candidate for his police-horse training program. Certain colts were selected each year to go through a little extra basic training in order to prepare them for potential careers as

law enforcement animals. David didn't need to take the training too far, as he knew that the mounted units liked to train horses in their own way, but he could do enough to make choosing easier when they came looking for potential remounts.

The extra training mainly involved exposing a young horse to as many new objects and situations as possible. Would he approach, and eventually step on, a tarp spread on the ground? Could he be ridden past farm machinery and vehicles without seeing a monster in every curve of the metal and growl of the engine? Tires, barrels, logs, other animals . . . they were all fair game.

By the time David got the call from the Toronto Police asking if he had any suitable remounts, Danny Boy was a steady, green-broke four year old and ready to be sold.

He was gentle in all ways, but not always quiet. He was playful and full of youthful spirit. He loved to run, and when he decided it was time to go, he would grab the bit, arch his powerful neck, and take his rider for the ride of his or her life. He never tried to buck anyone off, or hurt anyone. Occasionally he simply needed to remind people that life was not all work, work, work!

When Graham had been out a few weeks earlier to inspect the geldings, Danny Boy had tried his best to please and had been hard to spook when Graham deliberately rode him around items that would send many horses into fits. Danny Boy looked at all the scary things and sometimes approached them with caution, but he never refused and he never got upset. He had the perfect attitude and temperament for police work. That, and the fact that he was very well put together and solid enough to withstand just about anything that could come his way, convinced Graham this was the best horse of the three they'd seen.

Life would change drastically for the big, golden colt from that day forward. There would be no more pasture time, and hours of hard work every day. But his was an amiable, people-loving spirit, and he would adjust to the new routine more easily than most.

The adjustment started that very afternoon with a long trailer ride to the heart of the city of Toronto. Loading onto a trailer had been a part of Danny Boy's early training, but he had never taken an extended trip. He seemed unrattled by the experience of the two-hour journey, however, and he showed the same relaxed, good sense when he was moved into the roomy, freshly bedded box stall – stall number eight – that would be his home for the next five years. This, despite the fact that he had scarcely seen the inside of a stable in most of his life.

The time had come to join the world of men, and this big, golden colt had been chosen for a special assignment. He had joined the ranks of much-valued service animals – the guide dogs, search and rescue animals, RCMP and police horses and dogs, and the many others that work far more closely with humans than the average animal. He was chosen to make a difference in human life, to improve it and serve for it. All of this, he would do, and he would do it with the kindest spirit imaginable.

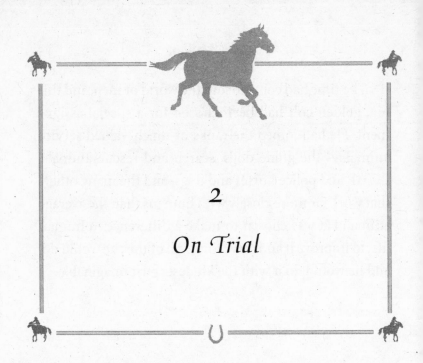

2

On Trial

The big Belgian cross colt would be on trial for the next two weeks, although Graham already felt positive there would be no need to send him back to Listowel. He would have to pass a veterinary inspection first, however, and prove himself steady enough during some initial tests and training to pass into full remount training. This testing began immediately.

It had been late in the afternoon when he had arrived at the Canadian National Exhibition Stables the day before, but he had been immediately immersed in the daily routines of a police horse.

He had been moved into his stall, and left to settle in – to nibble the top-quality hay that awaited him, drink from the clean pail of fresh, cool water that hung by his door, urinate in the aromatic shavings that cushioned the floor beneath his feet, and relax muscles tired from bracing against the unaccustomed movements of the trailer. The metal grating on the top half of his stall was left open so he could look around the stable and see the many other horses and people there. He watched with curiosity as men and women groomed and fed and cared for their mounts. Several officers came to visit this newest member of the Mounted and Police Dog Services. There were treats and pats, comments and nods of approval. It was very late before the final horses and riders had come in off their shifts and things had settled down for the night.

Now, at 6:30 the next morning, the stable was buzzing with activity again, as men and women began to arrive, drinking their coffees, yawning, calling their hellos in quiet morning voices, and getting ready for the day.

Morning feed came at 6:45. The other horses were obviously used to this as they were already up and leaning over their stall doors, nickering and pawing their impatience for a mouthful of sweet grain, hay, and a fresh drink. The colt leaned over his stall, too, curious about the activity and drawn by the sounds of grain being poured into pails and of rustling hay as flakes were torn from bales and tossed into stalls.

"You hungry, big boy?" asked a man who stopped and rubbed the colt's broad forehead before opening his stall door to give him his breakfast. The man stayed and watched for a few minutes, then he moved on to the next stall. Ronald Gilbert appreciated a good horse, and already, he had the feeling that this would be a good one. Something about those big, brown eyes. . . .

The stable remained active all morning, with twenty-eight stalls being cleaned, fresh bedding laid down, people coming and going, conversations growing louder and livelier as everyone woke up and got busy. There was always something to see, someone to visit with, a treat to be had . . . this was not a boring stable for a horse to live in.

Of course, the colt didn't know it, but he was being housed in the Horse Palace, at 140 Princes Boulevard, designed in 1931 to be one of the finest, and largest, equestrian facilities in Ontario, and possibly all of Canada. The stables had undergone extensive renovations just the year before and now held the entire Toronto Mounted Unit, which had previously been stabled in various locations around the city. The new facilities were clean and spacious and in keeping with the building's historical reputation as being the best ever built.

By 8:00 a.m., several of the officers were preparing their horses for the first work of the day. The officers and their equine partners would head out by 8:15 and patrol until noon, when the horses would come back for an afternoon meal and a rest. They would be back at work or in training by 3:15 and return again at 5:15 for a mid-afternoon feed at the end of their shift. Other horses would begin their shifts at 1:45 and would not finish for the day until 11:00 p.m. From Thursday to Sunday, teams would patrol the Entertainment District from 11:00 p.m. until 5:00 a.m.

He had no way of knowing it, but the colt had been selected for a job that would have him in constant human contact and on duty for long hours, usually working six or seven days in a row, with a two-day rest, and the best feed and care that could be provided as his only reward.

Graham Acott came to the gelding's stall after the colt had eaten his breakfast. With skilled and gentle hands he haltered the big horse and began to groom him, talking quietly to him all the while. It was the colt's first lesson as a police horse.

In few other places would the big horse find better care than where he was now. One of the main goals during the training of a police horse is to build confidence and trust, and to produce a partner that is accustomed to constant handling and teamwork. Graham had chosen this colt for his innate gentleness, and he would do everything he could to build on that good nature. The colt would never know a rough hand while in training or in service here. Graham knew that rough and hurried training methods would easily destroy a horse, but patience and kindness would bring out its best abilities.

Graham Acott's life was filled with horses, although it had not always been that way. Born and raised to British city life, he'd had only minimal exposure to the majestic animals in his early years. He joined the Metropolitan Police Service in London, England, as a young man and found himself irresistibly drawn to the Mounted Unit. There was nothing more impressive than the sight of the mounted officers patrolling the busy streets of London on their steadfast, courageous, and very beautiful animals. Life eventually led Graham to Canada, where he decided to pursue his interest, and he began a career that would span over two decades.

He joined the Toronto Mounted Unit in January 1986 and began his education to become a trainer from the start. For the first seven years of his service with the unit, Graham had worked as an apprentice trainer, learning the skills of the master trainers.

For a further three years, he had practiced his skills, with extra training from outside coaches. Finally, after ten years of riding, competing, training horses and riders under the guidance of others, and putting in thousands of hours, he had become a full-time trainer for the unit. Even now, he still recognized that every horse and rider had something to teach him, and he continued to receive instruction from outside coaches, always striving to be the best he could be for the benefit of the unit.

Every day, Graham was reminded of how blessed he was to have a job that allowed him to be around the animals he had come to love so much and the people who made the Mounted Unit so special. Today, as he curried the gelding's golden coat and watched the gentle, brown eyes follow his every move, he experienced that funny thrill of making a connection with a new animal. This, he loved.

The Horse Palace was equipped with a huge indoor training arena, as well as a large outdoor arena. Graham and the colt were soon kicking up the dust in the echoing dome of the indoor arena, other horses working around them, other trainers and their students moving through various stages of their career development. They would be spending countless hours there in the months to come.

Remount training normally takes six months to a year before a horse is considered ready to start work on the streets, depending on how much training it arrives with, its temperament, age, and many other factors. The fact that the colt was already green-broke was an advantage, as it saved two or three months in the training process and allowed him to be more accurately tested in these early, trial weeks.

Still, he was put back to basics on the lunge line. Graham had to be sure that the horse's early training had been complete and that what had been taught was thoroughly learned before he moved him onto more difficult tasks. Any step rushed without a complete mastery of the steps before could ruin a horse's confidence and set his whole training process back by weeks.

He was saddled now with a Universal Trooper saddle, a deep-seated cavalry-type saddle designed to keep the rider in place and comfortable during long hours of work. This he wore from the start, with side reins attached

during lunge line training. The change of saddle from the heavier Western style he had been accustomed to was not a problem for the colt, and he worked willingly that first day, readily moving through the steps of his work. He seemed to have a solid grounding in lunge work and a truly cooperative attitude. Graham was pleased. The first test had been passed.

The colt was back on the lunge later that day, this time with a rider in the saddle. Once again, he was put through his paces, but now taking his cues from both Graham, who was holding the line, and the rider on his back. This, too, caused the colt no great concern, and he did his best to do what was asked of him.

He was only worked for short spells that day, as he was not fit enough yet for a full schedule. Besides, Graham knew lunge work could be tedious for a young horse if done for too long. He would have his workload increased gradually, until he was in training for three or four hours a day, preparing to be under saddle for up to seven hours a day, once in full duty. This was not an easy job he'd been selected for, but it was a very special one.

The colt quickly adjusted to the daily routines and was soon joining in the chorus of nickers and door banging at meal times. He looked forward to the two or three times a day that he spent in the arena with Graham, and became excited as soon as he heard Graham's voice in the stable. Most of the training during the two weeks of his trial was focused around basic equitation skills – working in the arena on the lunge, or freely with a rider, practicing the walk, trot, canter, and reverse. Sometimes he worked alone, sometimes with other horses. Occasionally, Graham would bring in an obstacle – a barrel or a tarp or some other "spooky" thing to see how the colt would react.

By the end of the two weeks, there was no question. This colt had potential to be, not just a good police horse, but a great one. He was inquisitive, learned quickly, seemed nearly unflappable – which is rare in any young horse – and was an affectionate soul on top of it all. He got along well with both humans and the other horses, and this would be vital in the years to come.

Danny Boy passed a very thorough veterinary examination at the end of the two weeks, and the final approval was given. The sale was completed and officially recorded – *Remount 01/10/01, 4 yr. old chestnut gelding, 16.1hh, $5000.00 to David Carson, Listowel, ON*. The colt was now an official remount of the Toronto Police Department's extraordinary Mounted and Police Dog Services.

As a symbol of his new working status, his mane and forelock were roached (shaved like a buzz cut), although his thick blond tail was left unaltered. Only one thing remained to be done. The big golden horse needed a new name.

Occasionally, remounts are named through public contests, usually to commemorate special or historical events, but most of the horses on the unit are named by the officer-in-charge in a very unelaborate way. Almost always, they are given a recycled name, one that has been used for a horse in the past, and this is because there are stall nameplates and pieces of equipment already labeled that can be used again. It's a simple matter of economics.

The colt's naming was a quiet and simple event. The officer-in-charge selected a nameplate from the bin that everyone agreed was suitable for him. The nameplate was attached to stall number eight, and . . . he was Brigadier. The whole process spoke volumes about the life he had been selected for – a life of quiet duty and daily service, with very little special recognition, but steeped in tradition, history, and pride. A Brigadier is the fourth highest rank in the Canadian Armed Forces, a very important position to hold. Brigadier was a name to be lived up to.

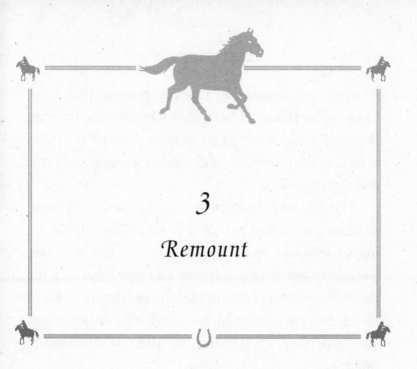

3
Remount

Brigadier was in full remount training now, spending time each day on the lunge line, long lines, and under saddle, learning to respond more and more subtly to the cues for the walk, trot, canter, and rein back. He also began to learn the sidepass and pivot on the rear and fore legs, both of which would be crucial in crowd control situations.

Graham did most of the early work with him, but as soon as he had shown that he had mastered his basic skills, different officers rode him each day, usually those who were not assigned to a specific horse of their own. These officers had all been through intensive training themselves and were taught to use a consistent style of riding, so the possibility of confusing a young horse was greatly reduced.

The frequent change in riders was considered beneficial, as a horse had to be able to do his job reliably, no matter who was on his back, because in this job there were frequent changes. It was also good training for the riders, who had to confidently handle any horse to which they were assigned, no matter how young or old, strong or lazy, cooperative, skittish, or stubborn it might be.

Every day Brigadier's confidence grew, along with his fitness level. As the routines became more ingrained, he became more energetic, and his personality began to shine through.

Graham wasn't the kind of person to show open emotion or favoritism toward the horses. They were like his children and he loved them all in a quiet, undemonstrative way. And like children, each horse had a unique personality and things that could be both challenging and endearing. Still, Graham couldn't help but be totally captivated by Brigadier's sweet nature. The playful antics that began to emerge as they went through their weeks together often made the reserved British trainer laugh out loud.

Brigadier could be very playful and full of "horse humor." The normally cooperative gelding would suddenly hold his head high above his handler's reach, making it nearly impossible to get a bridle on him. Sometimes he was nippy, taking every opportunity to annoy his handlers with his quick, playful bites, inviting them to join in a play-fight as though they were other horses. When working in the outdoor arena, he was prone to giving little bucks and sudden leaps – just for fun.

Occasionally, in the middle of a lesson, he would arch his heavy neck, shake the reins from his rider's grip, and break into a rollicking gallop. He was a freight train then, almost impossible to stop. To run free was the ultimate joy!

He could also be lazy and show a stubborn side. Then he would wear his riders out as they tried to get him to move out with a bit of energy. Many a rider ended their training session with cramped legs when Brigadier was bored with the routines and refused to work.

Most of the time, though, he was the most willing of students and an absolute gentleman. It wasn't long before Graham decided to include him in drills, or tactical maneuvers practiced in teams. The drills are similar to the musical ride put on by the RCMP, but they are more practical and work focused.

At least once a week, Graham and the other trainers would drill the remounts and the more experienced horses together in the arena. The horses and officers learned crowd control techniques, how to work obstacles and team formations and precision riding. Timing is essential in these types of movements, and that means good communication between the rider and his mount, and a horse that will respond immediately to a given cue. Brigadier seemed to enjoy these times with "the herd" and it was here that he demonstrated to Graham he was ready to begin the next step in his training.

During one of these early drill sessions, Graham set up a few obstacles for the teams to practice with. There was a teeter-totter bridge, which the horses had to step onto, allowing it to teeter to the other side as they walked across it, and step off, without panicking, of course. There were also tires on the ground, to work around and walk through, traffic flares, and a shallow water obstacle to cross. For the average horse, any one of these items could spell major trouble. For a police horse, they were all in a day's work and had to be accepted and dealt with.

The cold-blooded temperament of the grade horse, along with months of solid basic training and the development of absolute trust between the horse and rider becomes paramount during this type of work. Some horses handle it better than others. Some never do. Brigadier was a professional from the start.

Graham was riding Brig during that training session and was using him to demonstrate how to approach and handle these obstacles. As he explained to the newer officers, a horse won't necessarily see a tire on the ground as a tire on the ground. He only sees an unknown object as a possible predator waiting to prey on him, and his natural instinct tells him to get away from that potentially dangerous creature. In the wild, these are reasonable reactions necessary for survival. But on the streets of Toronto, the horse has to be able to override his instincts and not react to every object, every manhole, every plastic bag that blows in his path, or he would be a greater danger than help to citizens. Obstacle training was no small task for many horses and their human partners, and Brig was about to be tried out.

Brigadier had never seen many of these items before, and Graham realized this could end up being a very embarrassing deal for Brig and himself. But Graham

had great confidence in the big horse's abilities, so he walked him to the bridge and asked him to try.

Graham gave the gentle giant lots of rein, allowing him to stretch his neck and have a good look at the obstacle before him, but keeping just enough contact to regain control quickly if Brigadier became frightened. The trainer didn't push him, but gave him time to have a look, think about it, do things at his own pace.

Brigadier reached out with one of his massive hooves and struck at the bridge, as though testing its solidness. Then he moved forward and mounted the teetering structure with only the slightest quiver to show that the movement was worrying him. He stepped off the other side, and Graham fairly beamed with uncharacteristic pride. His praise was quiet, but deeply sincere. He had expected Brigadier to manage the exercise in reasonable form, but he was really quite amazed at how easily his young student had handled things. They proceeded through the remaining obstacles without hesitation or worry.

Brigadier was moving through his training quickly. He was working in a double bridle now (a bridle with two bits – the gentle snaffle, or bridoon, and the more severe curb bit, used when greater control was required), as all the police horses were trained to do. It was a big change from the mild snaffle he had worn until recently, but he accepted it easily, as usual.

Graham never rushed a young horse, but Brig seemed to understand what was required of him more quickly than average and only needed to be shown once or twice before he understood and tried his best to do things right. The rest was simply practice, which is the basis of all the mounted training. Repetition, until the cues and the corresponding actions become so ingrained as to be automatic. That way, in any situation the police are faced with, the chances of things happening as they need to are increased. An out-of-control horse that is not doing what it should and is simply reacting to its surroundings could cause enormous havoc in a peace-ful setting, and be downright dangerous in a crowded setting, such as a parade or a demonstration.

Brigadier was ready for the next stage in his training. Scare school! "Scare school" is a step up from obstacle training – basically the same thing, except the object is to present things that the horse might face while on patrol – things that could happen unexpectedly and scare him rather than obstacles that he could take time to explore and deal with slowly. Again, the focus was in training the horse to override his natural instinct of flight or fight, and to wait long enough for the rider to make the decision about whether the situation was safe or not and cue him accordingly. A horse that bolted, reared, or panicked at everything that came along would not make it as a police horse.

During these lessons, Graham would have other people suddenly appear and move toward the horse, waving flags, opening and closing an umbrella, making noise, flapping jackets, and presenting other sensory distractions that might cause problems. Brig was ridden through smoke and near fires and hissing flares, had blank guns fired beside him and over him, and people crowd him. It didn't take long before Brig would stand, imperturbable, no matter what came toward him, or what he was asked to do.

Graham began to take him out of the arena and onto quiet streets in the company of an older, more experienced horse and its rider. There he was exposed to even more scary stuff, from manholes to cement mixers, vehicles and sirens and people of all sizes, carrying all sorts of packages, bags, and other items. Sudden noises, bags blown in the wind, litter and garbage cans, signs and dogs on leashes and strays off leashes, parents pushing strollers and schoolyards full of active, noisy children. Brigadier was curious and cautious about it all, but never showed a sign of the panic that plagued some horses.

Brigadier was working hard, and at the end of a day's training, he seemed happy to be bathed, groomed, fed, and bedded down for the evening. He loved the constant conversations going on around the stable – the sounds were comforting and interesting. He began to recognize certain voices above others and watch for the people they belonged to.

Graham had become as familiar as anyone he had ever known, along with another man named Ted Gallipeau who had begun to ride him regularly, and was often the one to feed and care for him now. Ron Gilbert, the man who had brought him his first breakfast and often stopped by his stall to visit and bring little treats, was fast becoming a favorite of Brig's, as was a woman named Vicki Montgomery, another visitor and occasional caretaker, along with a few other regulars.

Sometimes in the evenings, Brigadier and the other horses would be turned loose in the big arena for some free play. Without access to paddocks, this was an important time of the day for many of the animals. It was a time to socialize, move unrestrained, roll . . . to be a horse.

Brigadier, still very young and full of life, seemed to enjoy this, but he did not seem to be missing his former pasture life at all. Some horses become restless and anxious, developing habits such as weaving, pawing, or chewing. Brigadier was settled and content, and could often be found with his head over his stall door, watching everything that was going on around him. Constantly curious, he kept himself entertained and attracted the attention of everyone passing by, ensuring that visits were frequent and treats plentiful. As it had been when he was a colt in Listowel, his gentle and naturally friendly temperament made him a favorite of many.

After seven long months of intensive daily training, Graham decided that Brigadier was ready to start working with the unit.

It was time to become a police horse.

4

Police Horse

*T*ed Gallipeau, a handsome, jovial, middle-aged officer, had expressed an interest in being partnered with the new horse, and Graham decided that Ted would be the most suitable choice. Young horses, new to the unit, are usually matched with experienced riders, and Ted had more experience than most people there. He had a firm, but gentle riding style that was perfect for the younger horses, and a calm, unshakable, yet playful personality that was a good fit with Brigadier's. Graham thought that Ted would be just the person to handle Brigadier during his stubborn streaks and playful moments, especially if they occurred while out on patrol.

Building the horse's confidence and obedience remained the key goal of training, and training would continue for the working life of the horse and rider. The basic training was complete, although Brigadier would continue to train in the arena at least once a week, but the real training would happen in the everyday events on the streets.

Ted and Brig worked together in the arena under Graham's guidance for two weeks before going out on their first patrol. This two-week period was a standard arrangement that all new partners went through to ensure that the match would work, that the horse was responding well to his new rider's commands, and that the rider was comfortable and confident on the mount he had been chosen for. It gave Ted a chance to figure out Brigadier's strengths and weaknesses, and Brig a chance to come to know the feel of Ted's cues, as every rider is slightly different. It was a bonding time.

By the time Ted fitted the official breastplate bearing the Toronto Mounted Police Unit's logo across his horse's broad, golden chest and prepared to ride out on their first shift, he had complete confidence in the rock-solid gelding. Despite his young age and inexperience, it seemed that nothing could frighten Brigadier.

The next several months were a time of growth and learning for Brigadier. He spent most of his days in the company of Ted. But with many more people than horses on the unit, unassigned officers, or those still in training, rode all of the horses in order to gain experience. Other riders, like Vicki Montgomery and Ron Gilbert, had plenty of experience but no partner, and they both liked having a chance to ride a new young horse like Brigadier.

Bonds ran deep between the horses and their human partners, and the atmosphere in the Horse Palace was one of friendship and caring. Often the police officers spend as much, or even more time with their equine partners than they do with their own families. For Ted Gallipeau, a horse lover to the core, these bonds ran especially deep. The horses were no less than family, needing all of his care and attention. He loved each one, but he grew to love Brigadier greatly.

Ted and Brigadier teamed up once a week with Vicki Montgomery and an older, experienced horse named Toby. The more experienced horse and human were helpful in teaching both Vicki and Brigadier the skills they needed, in a calm and supportive setting. Vicki loved working with the good-natured older man and she learned a great deal from watching him handle his young mount. There was affection in every action and a concern for the comfort and welfare of the animal that inspired her. She watched as Brigadier gave back with unshakable devotion, and Vicki was moved by the bond she witnessed between them.

Brigadier had a gentleness that touched everyone who knew or met him. Of all the horses in the stable, he was the best with kids and during public demonstrations of any kind, he was the one who received the most kisses and hugs from the children. He would lower his enormous blazed head to their level, as if to get a better look at his young fans, while they clambered around his soup-bowl sized feet, patted and kissed his nose, and stroked his thick neck. Brig would remain still and careful to never hurt a hair on their heads – or their toes. He seemed to genuinely enjoy the times when he was able to visit with children and, over the years, he would touch the hearts of many as he worked the streets of Toronto.

Ted always laughed at how women also seemed to be drawn to him – to "those big brown eyes" and the beautiful thick, blond tail. The golden giant just seemed to bring out the best in people.

"He's quite a chick magnet," Vicki would tease. Ted always insisted that *he* was the chick magnet, and that Brigadier was just an excuse for the women to get closer to him, but everyone knew better!

As his confidence grew, so did his playfulness. He could try Ted at times, slipping out of his stall during feeding time to visit or create a little havoc with the other horses, nipping while being groomed, spooking his stablemates during drills by giving loud farts, followed by playful squeals and bucks, or simply refusing to cooperate and work. Ted would just laugh and gently but firmly push Brig to do what he needed to do. He knew that once they were out on the street, Brigadier would be the most dependable of partners and the fooling around would stop. Brig had plenty of spirit, but even more sense.

Until it was time to head back to the barn, that is. It didn't take long before Brig had the routine figured out and as soon as it was time to quit work for the day, he would come to life, gigging and prancing the whole way back, eager for his bath and a good meal. Given his head, he would have galloped home at the end of each shift. "Homing" became Brig's signature bad habit, and one that each of his riders would try to cure, without success.

When they turned him toward home, Brig had no time to waste!

During these months, Ted fell completely in love with the big, golden gelding, and he wasn't the only one. Vicki volunteered to ride or care for him when Ted was not available, and loved to brush out his thick, silky tail. Ron Gilbert continued to visit the big gelding almost daily, bringing special treats of Quaker Instant Apple & Cinnamon cereal that Brig loved to lick from his hand. He often rode and cared for Brigadier, privately hoping to be partnered with him someday. Everyone in the stable was touched by Brig's big heart and sweet personality, but Ted, Ron, and Vicki stood out as ones who touched his gentle heart in return.

5
Ron's Big Boy

In the summer of 2002, Ted was transferred to the Quarter Master's position in the unit, meaning he would have to give up his regular patrol shift for duties at the stable office. He and Ron Gilbert were longtime friends, and Ron's affection for the gelding had not gone unnoticed. Ron had the experience and the personality to continue bringing the young horse along in his job and Ted made the request to have Ron take over for him.

Ron was delighted when Ted offered his partner to him. As much as he had hoped for it, he had never really expected it to happen. He wasn't even sure why he felt so strongly about this particular horse. He had been with the Toronto Police for almost thirty years, most of that time spent with the Mounted Unit and he had ridden many a good horse over that time. There was just something about Brigadier that had captured his attention from the very first day he'd seen him.

An animal lover to the core, Ron was always interested in the new four-legged recruits when they came in. Right away, he had seen something beyond the solid, massive build, the straight legs, and well-formed neck and head. There was something about this horse's eyes – an expression that was hard to put into words.

It didn't take long before Brigadier became known as Ron's Big Boy, and over the course of the months and years to follow, Ron and the golden giant of a horse enjoyed a very special friendship. Other officers rode him in drills and training, but it was clear that this was Ron's pet and partner. Theirs was a friendship that would last for the next four years, until tragedy would tear them apart.

Ron and Brigadier spent countless hours together in those years, patrolling the parks, Lake Ontario area, and the Rouge Valley in all kinds of weather, controlling crowds during demonstrations and parades, doing traffic duty, searching for missing people, and, more than most other horses on the unit, participating in public relations events. He was a beautiful prince of a horse, and drew people to him like a rock star. People always liked to visit the police horses, but when Brigadier was around, it was a whole different affair. He was the public's horse as much as he was the Unit's, and he seemed to genuinely enjoy the extra attention he earned in that role. Many a child sat on his broad back and felt his warm breath on their cheeks as they kissed his satiny muzzle.

Ron and Brigadier filled their days in service, duty, and comradeship. A mounted policeman puts in a long, hard day, along with his equine partner. Besides the six or more hours spent on patrol, there are stalls to be cleaned, animals to be groomed and cared for, tack and equipment to be kept in immaculate condition, paperwork to be done, and training time to be spent in the arena. It is a full and demanding job, but the Mounted Unit officers know they are blessed with one of the most rewarding and fulfilling jobs they could hope to have.

Of course, the horses have no choice about whether they would do such a difficult job or not, but they are loved and well cared for while in service, and they perform an invaluable role, taking the place of ten to fifteen men on foot. Ron always felt perfectly safe on

Brigadier's back, confident that his equine partner would take good care of him. People tended to show a great deal of respect for a police officer who rode up on such a massive horse as Brigadier, and he and Ron were rarely troubled by people challenging their authority.

Brigadier wormed his way into every area of Ron's life, both at work and at home. Ron took stories of the days he spent with Brig home to his wife and children, until he was as much a part of their lives as he was of Ron's. They worked together, played together, and even competed as a team. Ron's wife and children often visited Brigadier at the stable and always came to watch special events like parades, competitions, or other public relations events. He was family to them all.

Brigadier, a gentleman to the core most of the time, occasionally still loved to cut loose and run. The horse that sometimes had to be pushed to move out in the arena would respond to the lightest touch while out in the park and would soon be carrying Ron on a heart-stopping gallop of pure power. In the waters of Lake Ontario, when Ron let him run along the shoreline during hot summer days, Brigadier would leap through the waves, seeming to delight in making the splashes as big as possible, soaking himself and Ron from head to foot. These were among Ron's favorite times with the golden giant.

In the show ring, they turned out to be as formidable a team as they were working partners.

To encourage continued training and development of officers and their horses, and to provide opportunities for friendly competition and connecting between officers of the various Mounted Units across North America, Mounted Police Competitions are held each year. These begin at the local level, with the unit conducting its own competitions several times per year. Winners at this level can compete at the Nationals, which are held in a different part of North America each year.

There are three main types of classes to be tried. In the uniform class, officers and horses are judged on their turnout. The equitation class judges the horse and rider on basic training movements, such as the walk, trot, canter, reverse, and sidepass, and variations of these.

The most popular, and probably most important, is the obstacle class, which is based on situations an officer and his mount might face on actual patrols in the city, sometimes including a "fleeing felon" segment. This is a timed event, not only judged by how well the team negotiates the obstacles, but by how quickly they do it.

Occasionally, there will be a Troop Drill and Police Class, where drill teams can demonstrate their skills. The Ride and Shoot, in which a rider has to shoot four targets while riding at a canter, is always challenging, but popular.

Ron had been competing in these competitions for years, and decided that it might be fun, and good training, to try Brigadier out in this type of activity. He had already proven that he was a natural in obstacle work, which is a big element in the competitions, but they would have to work for the equitation part of it, as this was when Brigadier tended to get stubborn.

They began training for their first competition within a few months of becoming partners. Brigadier, as he always had, took the increased work in stride, trying hard to do what Ron asked of him. Before long, they were side passing, backing through tricky patterns, jumping and negotiating obstacles, plus much, much more. By October of their first year together, they had won their local level shows with style, and were on their way to Fredericksburg, VA., for the National Mounted Police Competition. There, Brig shone, along with a few of his stablemates who had also taken the journey, and the group came home four days later, well placed in the standings.

They made it to the Nationals the next year also, and traveled to Lexington, KY., to compete. This time, they did even better. Brigadier blew the competition away. Now a mature six year old, Brigadier showed them all how a great police horse can handle himself, even under the pressure of smoke clouds, gunfire, obstacles of all sorts, crowds of pushy people, and other horses who were losing their cool around him. There would be no fooling around during these important days. Brigadier seemed to sense the seriousness that was required of him, and he gave his all. He worked like a champion, and at the end of the competition, he had earned that title.

When the team began the journey back to the Horse Palace, they had one more member than when they arrived. The championship prize for the competition was more than just a ribbon or a plaque to hang on the wall, or a new cooler for the winning horse, although these things were coming home, too. Brig had won the Toronto Mounted Unit a new horse – a big gray gelding called Blue Moon. Blue Moon would move into the stall right next to Brigadier's and begin basic training immediately.

Brig and Ron would make it to Nationals one more time, in 2004. They wouldn't have to travel so far this time as the National Competition was held in Kingston,

Ontario, that year. Once again, the team did well, although they did not match their 2003 Championship performance.

For Ron, the championship was a bonus. The real reward came in the time he was able to spend with his remarkable partner, in the everyday work and interactions with the people on the streets. The competitions were always great fun, but Brigadier didn't need a trophy to prove he was a champion. He proved it daily. Still, the title was special and Ron was proud of him!

Brigadier's ability to touch people's lives never wavered during these years of service and work with Ron: the teenagers who visited the Unit as a class and sat on his back, experiencing the thrill of such a powerful yet gentle animal beneath them, the tiny children who continued to be Brig's favorites, the intrepid photographer, Anne de Haas, who photographed the horses of the Unit and was particularly moved by the beautiful gelding. All who met him felt the touch of his spirit.

During the winter of 2005, a member of the Emergency Tactical Force (ETF) visited Brigadier regularly. Tim Crone became acquainted with the golden giant while completing a fifteen-week training course, in hopes of joining the Mounted Unit. Brigadier was soon a definite favorite of Tim's. Twelve years of service with the stressful tactical team had made Tim a rather serious soul, but Brigadier found a way to make him smile and laugh every time they were together.

Tim loved to visit the horses, finding a peacefulness and calm in their presence that provided a well-needed relief from the mental burdens of his job. Tim found this to be especially true of Brigadier, who seemed to listen with his whole being and absorb the tension from the tired man's body. Brigadier was generous with his affections, and something about looking into those deep brown eyes, or having that great blazed head resting against his chest for a few moments could ease Tim's mind like very little else could.

Tim passed the training course, but his strong leadership skills were more needed in the ETF at that time, so he returned to his usual post and wait for the call to join the Mounted Unit. In the meantime, he would become a regular visitor and could often be found near Brigadier's stall.

Ted remained a big fan of Brigadier's, as did Vicki Montgomery, who cared for him and rode him whenever Ron could not. Ron trusted her with his Big Boy, and that trust was not taken lightly. Vicki loved Brigadier as much as anyone there, and was pleased whenever she had the opportunity to work and be with him.

Other officers rode him at times: Graham Acott, to monitor his training, Staff Inspector Bill Wardle, for the occasional PR event, and other officers for training and practice. But most of the time, it was Ron and Brigadier, and it was hard to imagine them apart.

6

A Third and Final Partner

Becoming a member of the elite Mounted and Police Dog Service involves a lengthy and rigorous journey. Only First Class Constables (officers who have been in regular police duty for at least three years) may apply. They apply personally to the Unit Commander, and if they are considered suitable candidates – if they appear to be of the required body type (under one hundred and eighty pounds and fit), and have a personality suited to working with animals in high-stress situations (calm, with a sense of humor, not prone to nervousness or angry outbursts), and a sincere desire to work with the Unit, then they are invited to fill out a Mounted Unit application.

If the application is accepted, the officer must pass a physical fitness test at the Police College. Mounted Unit officers are expected to have and to maintain an above-average fitness level. Their personal employment record is also reviewed. They must have an exemplary service record to be considered for the Unit.

If they make it this far, they are invited to attend a fifteen-week equitation course. A mounted officer takes over the recruit's regular fieldwork for the fifteen weeks, which ensures that Mounted officers continue to stay up to date on their police training, while regular officers have a chance to be trained for the Mounted Unit.

Recruits endure grueling training on horseback, along with half days in the classroom, and they must pass an extensive equitation test before being allowed to write their final exams.

For those who survive the whole process, a Mounted Unit diploma is earned at a formal graduation ceremony . . . and then they go back to their regular jobs and wait, hopefully, for the call to join the unit.

In May 2005, a young officer named Kevin Bradfield became one of the newest members of Toronto's Mounted Unit. He had grown up with two desires; to be a policeman and to ride. He had been riding all of his life, and knew that a job that combined both of his passions would be perfect for him. During the fifteen-week training course, he was exposed to most of the horses on the unit. Brigadier immediately stood out for him.

Brigadier was an imposing-looking animal – a broad, muscular, golden tank with a jagged white blaze, four tall white stockings and a luxurious, streaked tail. You couldn't help but take notice of him. Kevin soon learned, though, that he was as gentle a horse as he would ever ride, and he, like everyone else who knew him, quickly chose him as his favorite mount.

Ron liked Kevin right away. He enjoyed the younger officer's quick sense of humor, cocky confidence, and gentleness with the horses. Ron and Kevin shared a love of animals, and horses in particular, and it showed in the affection they were not afraid to demonstrate toward their equine partners.

Brigadier suddenly found himself enjoying the attentions of yet another officer, and he liked it. He seemed to connect with Kevin from the start, and would come to the front of his stall and watch the man's movements around the stable as soon as he heard Kevin's voice. The apples and carrots Kevin always had hidden in his pockets probably had much to do with this, along with the young man's cheerful personality and ability to know just the right places to scratch.

Kevin had been on horseback for most of his life and tended to ride a little aggressively and fearlessly. Brigadier was the first to bring the confident young man down a notch and start retraining him toward a more cautious, "city-riding" style.

In the midst of his fifteen-week training session, Kevin earned his official Toronto Police spurs. He was eager to try them out, and happened to be riding Brigadier that day. Brigadier was being a little lazy, and Kevin was happy to have a new kind of "gas pedal" to try out on him. So, when he asked for a canter and Brigadier did not respond quickly, Kevin lightly touched the spurs to the big horse's sides.

Brigadier sprung to life and broke into a gallop, arching his powerful neck and picking up speed. He was soon flying around the arena with Kevin hanging on for dear life. When Kevin finally regained control several minutes later, he was winded and his heart was pounding, but he immediately began to laugh. "Okay, I get the picture," he said, as he patted Brig's neck. "No spurs for you!"

Lessons with Brig, time on the streets with Greg Ladner, one of the most experienced Senior Mounted

Officers, and observing the care that this legendary rider took with every step on Toronto's slippery concrete streets gradually changed Kevin's riding style to one of greater awareness, caution, and care. The changes did not go unnoticed.

Near the end of that year, Ron was asked if he would be interested in working with Blue Moon, the horse he and Brig had won. Blue Moon had been in training for a long time, but was ready for a permanent, experienced rider who could bring him along. It would mean letting someone else partner with Brigadier. Ron was reluctant to do that, but he knew that Brig had gained enough experience to be reliable in the hands of any one of the capable riders on the unit. He was interested in the big gray gelding they had shipped in from Kentucky. He wasn't as quiet as Brig, but he was a nice horse with a lot of potential, and he would be a fun challenge to bring along.

It was a very hard decision for Ron, but when 2006 began, Brigadier had a new rider. Ron requested that Kevin be given the partnership and, despite the fact that Kevin was one of the newest members on the unit, this was granted. Brigadier would be the one to teach Kevin, and Blue Moon, the ropes out on the streets and parkways.

For the next five weeks, Brigadier and Kevin were nearly inseparable. Brig was Kevin's first official mount, and, like many firsts in life, this was special. Brig stood for everything Kevin valued and strove toward in his work. He was brave and steady and had incredible strength of character, while being remarkably friendly and gentle at the same time. In this way, they were well matched.

Right from the start, the other officers were quick to tell Kevin how lucky he was to have Brigadier. Vicki had remained one of his biggest fans over the years, always covering his care when Ron wasn't around and riding him whenever she had the opportunity. Many other officers had also hoped to be awarded the partnership with the handsome horse. But there were no hard feelings. Everyone got to ride all of the horses and everyone was happy for Kevin when they found out about Ron's request. They all respected Ron, and knew that if he chose Kevin for Brig, that the choice was not made lightly. It was the right choice.

Kevin didn't need to be told he was lucky. He knew it every time he walked into Brigadier's stall and was greeted by those gentle eyes and soft nickers.

Kevin would sometimes come into Brigadier's stall and find the big horse stretched out on his side, fully relaxed. Most other horses would jump to their feet at

the approach of someone in their stall, but Brig would simply raise his head to see who it was, then lay it back down in the shavings and continue resting. Kevin would go in and sit on Brig's side and talk to him, ask him how he was doing, if he was ready to go to work. Brigadier would watch him and breath his soft, puffing breaths and listen to his partner's deep voice as it rolled soothingly over him. This became a regular ritual with the pair – a quiet time of trust and bonding, and it was the thing Kevin would remember most fondly about his time with the great horse in the future.

When Brigadier finally decided that he was ready to get up, he would heave his great mass onto his feet, shake a layer of shavings from his back, then stand and look at Kevin calmly. Kevin had to laugh almost every time. The splendid prince of a horse would be covered from head to hoof with manure stains and wood chips. His whole look was one of rumpled morning bed-head. Brigadier was not a tidy horse! A trip to the wash rack was required almost daily to get Brig looking his professional best. Brigadier loved his baths, and Kevin loved him.

On patrol, they were just as close, a jovial pair, on the streets of Toronto looking for the next smile, wave, or conversation with people of all walks of life. As they paused beside the street-side metal fence of a daycare center, dozens of little children would run up, squealing their joy at seeing the big horse, and sticking their hands through the fencing to pat the satiny nose that stretched down toward them.

Staff Inspector Bill Wardle recognized the quality of the great golden horse as a public relations ambassador and rode him to events occasionally, especially when a particularly personable and gentle animal was required. PR was an important part of Bill's job.

Early in February 2006, he asked Anne de Haas, the unit's official photographer, to come and do special portrait shots of the Unit's horses for a gallery he planned to include in one of the hallways.

Anne set up her equipment in the dimly lit arena, with the smell of dust and hay and horses all around her. For now, she and Bill decided to do the horses whose names had historical significance, as there were too many to get through in one day. Over the course of a few hours, the horses were brought in wearing only their halters. For Anne, it was a little nerve-racking. The horses were used to being turned out in the arena for playtime at that hour, so they came in energetically and expectantly, and then had to stand still mere feet from her expensive equipment. By the time they had worked through the list, she was tired.

Just as they thought they were finished, Brigadier was led in. Anne had run across him before – he was one of the most photographed horses on the unit, in fact, and she had a soft spot for him, like most of his acquaintances. He was one of the most striking horses she had ever seen, but Brigadier wasn't on the list to be photographed that night. Bill had decided it would be a good idea to have a portrait of the champion "people's horse" for PR purposes, though, and so they did him as well. Little did they know just how famous that spur-of-the-moment portrait would become.

7

The Most Tragic Night

Friday, Feb. 24, 2006

Kevin Bradfield and Brigadier, Ron Gilbert and Blue Moon, and two other officers and their mounts were on Community Patrol on Lawrence Avenue, between Kingston and Morningside Roads in Scarborough. They had paired off earlier and, as usual, Kevin and Ron were riding together, chatting, joking, talking about their families and their horses. Their winter uniforms were only just keeping the cold at bay. They were thankful for the slightly warmer weather – it had been frigid just the week before.

They had already been riding for three hours, patrolling local greenbelts, plazas, and schoolyards, making the police presence known in the areas frequented by drug dealers and gang members. It was a typical Friday night, with people starting to move around the city in search of entertainment. They investigated any suspicious-looking vehicles or people, and they chatted with community members and the young people who were beginning to gather as the evening grew deeper.

It was nearly 7:00 p.m. when Ron and Kevin were riding past a TD Canada Trust automated teller machine (ATM) drive-through on the southwest corner of Kingston Road and Lawrence. A concerned citizen approached them to report that a man at the bank machine was upset and acting aggressively toward another driver, swearing and shouting at him.

Kevin guided Brigadier as close to the van as he could get, but the machine wall blocked his way, preventing him from investigating more fully. He asked the man to pull over once he was finished his banking business so that they could talk. Ron was nearby and the two other officers, McCarthy and Stravakis, had just come into view at the far end of the street.

The man did not pull over as requested, but drove quickly away. Ron and Kevin raised eyebrows at each other and Kevin grinned. There was nothing they could do about it, and the man wasn't wanted for anything, so they let him go and resumed their patrol, crossing Lawrence Avenue.

Less than a minute later, the van was speeding toward them at top speed, and before Kevin and Brigadier could get out of the way, it struck them. Kevin was thrown from his partner's back and lay, stunned, and in pain on the sidewalk. Brigadier crumpled where he was hit, his two front legs shattered by the impact. The man in the van sped away.

Ron and the two other officers were on the scene immediately, calling for assistance and an ambulance for Kevin. Ron went to Brigadier's head and tried to offer comfort to his friend, who was wild-eyed with pain and fear. He held him down as the giant horse thrashed and tried to rise on legs that would never support him again. Ron was so shocked and horrified that all he could concentrate on was consoling Brig as best he could, minute by excruciating minute.

Citizens held Blue Moon and one of the other horses while the third was ridden off to bring the four-horse trailer, which was parked nearby. Once the trailer was on site, the three horses were secured in their stalls. By then, Kevin was on his way to the hospital in an ambulance. The scene was chaotic and horrific. The media began to arrive, bystanders were crying at the sight of the fallen animal. Crowd control became an issue.

The police dispatcher notified the stable and PC Chris Heard was sent with a two-horse trailer and a six-car police escort to be ready to transport Brigadier to the Veterinary College in Guelph if emergency medical treatment was deemed possible.

Bill Wardle was contacted at his home and rushed to the scene, arriving around 7:20 p.m. Brigadier was in severe distress, with several officers now holding him down and shock beginning to show in his pain-filled eyes. After assessing the severity of Brigadier's horrific injuries and consulting with the veterinary surgeon by phone, the inspector made the painful decision to have Brig euthanized. There was no way to mend two broken legs. His suffering needed to end.

PC Heard was sent back to the stable with the other three horses, Blue Moon, Elvis, and Viscount. Normally quiet and easy to transport, the trio was upset and unruly in the trailer. Blue Moon was so overwrought that Chris had to stop three times to calm him down and prevent him from kicking the trailer to pieces.

The vet was forty-five minutes away, so Bill decided to have the Emergency Tactical Force come instead. Brig's old friend, Tim Crone, took the call and felt the first pangs of anguish as he was told they were needed to deal with a police horse that was down and suffering severe traumatic injuries.

Tim drove to the scene as fast as he could, the feeling of foreboding intensifying with each passing moment. His footsteps slowed as he approached the scene and his heart pounded. The first thing he saw was the thick blond tail, and he knew which horse this was. It took all of his training to hold himself together and do the job that needed to be done, especially when he saw Ron, shocked and grieving, tenderly holding the head of his Big Boy, and the damaged breastplate with the Toronto Police crest stretched taut across the broad, torn chest of this beautiful horse.

Neither Ron or Tim or any of the other officers present attempted to hide their pain or their tears as ballistics shields were put into place around the scene and the public was moved away.

At approximately 7:50 p.m., nearly an hour after he had been run down, Tim whispered good-bye to his friend one last time, and then did the hardest thing he'd ever had to do during his long career. He aimed his gun and put Toronto's most beloved police horse out of his misery.

8

An Incredible Love

To say that the Mounted Unit was thrown into a state of grief would be an understatement. Everyone on the unit had been touched by Brigadier's spirit at one time or another, and losing him was not simply the loss of a horse, but the loss of one of their own.

Ron and the other officers were taken to 43 Division to provide statements that would assist in the arrest of the man who had run Brigadier and Officer Bradfield down so brutally.

A description of the van was posted, and witnesses were asked to call Crime Stoppers.

Kevin, it was soon reported, was in stable condition at Scarborough Centenary hospital with injuries to his ribs, back, and neck. Brigadier had taken the brunt of the hit, and in doing so, had undoubtedly saved his rider's life. Telling Kevin that his partner had been killed was one of the hardest tasks the rest of the unit had to face. Not surprisingly, his sadness was profound.

Ron was also extremely upset by the incident. Seeing his longtime partner mown down, then holding him and seeing his pain as he lay, suffering in the street, was almost more than he could bear. He was not ashamed of the tears that flowed that night or in the days to follow. He had lost a dear friend and it affected him deeply.

Vicki was at home recovering from dental surgery when she received the news. She too was devastated, not only for Brigadier, but for the men she knew would be hurt the most by his sudden, tragic death.

Ted and Graham were also contacted at home and were both profoundly shocked and saddened by the news and the footage they saw on TV.

Anne de Haas arrived home shortly after the incident occurred and was greeted by her son, David, calling her to come see the news. "Something has happened to one of the police horses," he said.

She rushed to the television, expecting to see a newscaster speaking of the incident, but found, instead, horrifying live coverage of the golden giant thrashing in pain and being held down by several officers. The image was burned into her mind, and in the days to come, she would wish she had never seen it.

Bill Wardle had the same thought. Brigadier was the people's horse, and he hated the idea of those images being the last they would have of him. He phoned Anne right away and asked if the portrait photo she had taken was available to send to headquarters. She e-mailed it to him immediately, and it was this image of a powerful, gentle, beautiful Brigadier that was released to the media when he and Police Chief William Blair returned to the scene to provide a statement a short time later. Soon world-wide attention had focused on the event.

In his statement, Chief Blair announced that the force would be investigating the incident very aggressively, and that he felt "the entire city of Toronto will be touched by the loss of this animal."

Later that night, Dirk Sankersingh was arrested and charged with dangerous driving causing bodily harm and failing to remain at the scene of an accident. Many would protest the lightness of these charges. Many more were calling it murder. Service animal protection would become a major issue in the weeks to follow.

News spread very quickly, and it was soon evident that the members of the Mounted Unit were not the only ones feeling grief and loss. Poems, letters, photos, and cards began pouring in from all across North America, many from children who had met, touched, and been touched by the gentle police horse. The huge outpouring of sympathy and anger was unexpected and overwhelming. Brigadier had been greatly loved, and the whole country felt the loss, although nowhere more than in the city of Toronto.

The first thing to cross Ted Gallipeau's desk on his first shift back to work was a card from one of the many hundreds of children who had met Brigadier and experienced his gentle kindness. It showed a picture of a big brown horse with white markings and quotes inside describing Brigadier and the sadness she felt at his death. Police duties continued with the Mounted Unit present for a demonstration in downtown Toronto, but Ted, along with many others, found it hard to get through that day . . . every time he thought of that card, he found himself fighting tears.

The feeling of immense grief hung over the entire stable. Brigadier's stall stood empty and quiet. His gleaming halter hung by his nameplate. Even the other horses were quieter than usual and seemed to sense that one of their herd was missing.

As the day wore on, the cards and letters of condolence and flowers continued to be delivered to the stable. Brigadier's empty stall was soon decorated with symbols of love and caring, and for the members of the Mounted Unit, this was incredibly comforting and healing.

By Monday, arrangements had been made for a memorial service to be held on Thursday at a funeral home near the scene of the incident. The flag over the police stables on the grounds of the Canadian National Exhibition flew at half-mast all that week, as it would have for any fallen officer.

Toronto's Mayor, David Miller, made a public statement regarding Brigadier's death, expressing his shock and sadness and good wishes for Kevin Bradfield and the entire Mounted Unit.

"Brigadier was a much-loved and irreplaceable member of our Mounted Unit and his loss leaves within the unit a void both emotionally and operationally that will take time to heal and will be difficult to fill.

The death of any member of the Toronto Police Service in the line of duty is tragic and unfortunate. On behalf of all Torontonians, I extend condolences to all members of the Service and in particular the Mounted Unit where the loss of a friend and colleague is sure to hit hardest."

By Tuesday, it was evident that they would need a bigger space to hold the memorial as so many people were indicating a desire to attend. The outpourings of sympathy and love continued, and the police service realized that they needed to make this a memorial for the people, as well as for the police force. The Ricoh Coliseum was booked for Monday at 10:00 a.m.

Monday, March 6, 2006, will stand out in many people's minds as a special day, a day when an animal received the same hero's sendoff that would have been awarded any human who had worn the same symbol of service and had made "the ultimate sacrifice." It was a day when the Toronto Police Service and the city demonstrated its belief that there is no set value on life, be it human or animal, and no real difference between a human hero or animal hero. It was a noble day.

Hundreds of dignitaries and police officers, including members of various Mounted Units and the Royal Canadian Mounted Police, were joined by well over a thousand civilians to pay their respects to the horse they had grown to love.

Not everyone who wanted to be there, could be. Vicki Montgomery and several other officers came to work that morning, planning to attend the memorial, but were called out on a search for a missing child. The child was found, fortunately, but the day was bitter-sweet for the officers called to duty, as they experienced the sadness of not being able to say their good-byes, along with the relief of recovering the child and pride in a job well done.

The Service's pipe band and the Chief Ceremonial Unit led the memorial as four officers and canines from the Police Dog Service along with eight mounted officers took their places. The Master of Ceremonies, Gary Grant, welcomed five speakers to the podium seats and acknowledged the many dignitaries in attendance, as well as the citizens of Toronto and beyond who had chosen to be there.

On display were Brigadier's saddle, bridle, and breastplate, the beautiful portrait taken by Anne de Haas just before his death, and three red roses, in honor of his three main riders, Ted, Ron, and Kevin.

The chaplain of the Police Service, Rev. Walter Kelly, spoke of the way animals touch our lives, and in particular, horses: "There is something about the majestic

horse that inspires all of us." He spoke of the bond that forms between the horse and rider, a bond so evident in the day-to-day lives of the members of the Mounted Unit. He read a quote, which expressed it so well: "Riding is a partnership. The horse lends you his strength, speed, and grace, which are greater than yours. For your part, you give him your guidance, intelligence, and understanding, which are greater than his. Together, you can achieve a richness that, alone, neither can."

Kevin Bradfield, looking very young, and doing his best to contain his emotions, spoke of his friend and the bond they shared. Through his tears, he recalled special memories of Brigadier and expressed how thankful he was to be able to say good-bye to his partner. As he took his seat, his fellow officers, and all present, rose in a standing ovation. Brigadier was not the only member of that partnership to have earned the great affection of the people and the Unit.

PC Michael Stravakis, who had been riding with Kevin on that awful night, read a poem he had written about Brigadier, a beautiful tribute to the great horse:

"Your might was fearsome, though your manner gentle.
Authority rang with each step of your shod hooves,

But the innocence in your eyes was inviting to those
    without malice.
How many thousands of hands have stroked your
    soft muzzle!
Proud officers were prouder still, when they could see
The world from atop your shoulders.
Your purpose: 'Preserve the Peace,'
Your practice: winning the tender affection of chil-
    dren and adults."

Staff Inspector Bill Wardle, still feeling the impact of
that terrible night, still having difficulty putting the horrific images of Brig's final moments behind him, spoke
also of the bond that occurs between horses and riders
on the Unit and how very much they become a part of
the officers' families. He spoke to those who questioned
the need for a formal memorial service for a "mere
animal," as of course, there had been some criticism of
the force's decision to have such a large service. He spoke
of the need for all of those involved that night, the riders
and other officers, the paramedics, firefighters, civilians
who had assisted, and people who had seen the footage
on television, to be able to remember Brigadier with
affection, respect, and dignity. It was the beginning of
being able to heal and move forward.

Finally, Chief of Police, William Blair paid tribute to Brigadier and the members of the Mounted Unit, praising the work of the Mounted officers in the city, and speaking of how encouraging the public's support had been in the past week to the Unit and the entire Police Service. "In the aftermath of such a sad event, it is very encouraging to . . . be reminded of the special relationship that exists between the people of Toronto and all of the members of our service. . . ."

The pipers concluded with a medley of musical ride and drill pieces in honor of Brigadier, who had been a member of the drill team. While they played, video footage and still images of Brigadier and the Mounted Services were projected on a large screen – footage that brought many to tears.

Those final images of Brigadier were not ones of pain and suffering, but of affection and patience, playfulness and service, gentleness and love. The pictures showed the Brigadier that was – simple, honest, and sweet – just as he should be remembered.

9

Remembering a Hero

For the public, and for members of the Police Service, especially the Mounted Unit, the weeks to follow were a time of healing.

For some, this came in the form of poems, paintings, plaques, sculptures, letters, drawings, and other expressive forms that soon filled the lobby of the Horse Palace. So many people had been touched by Brigadier's spirit, and now these same people were giving back to the men and women left behind.

For others, healing came in taking action to try to improve the way the legal system dealt with acts of deliberate cruelty toward animals, and in particular, law enforcement animals.

Although Brigadier was the first horse to be intentionally harmed while in service, he was not the first animal. Several dogs had been severely injured or killed while working alongside their human partners. Every loss was devastating to the people who had worked with these highly trained and remarkable creatures, and their deaths left a huge gap in the police units they worked for. However, the people responsible for their deaths seldom received more than a light fine for their actions, since animals in Canada receive very little legal protection.

At the time of Brigadier's death (as they still do now), all animals in Canada fell under property laws, making it extremely difficult for law enforcers to come up with serious charges to lay against offenders. Only cattle have any protection under the Criminal Code of Canada.

Since 1999, concerned citizens and politicians had been attempting to pass a Bill thus creating a new law that would offer ALL animals legal protection under the Criminal Code, with a special section of this Bill dealing with law enforcement animals. Within hours of his death, this Bill was renamed Brigadier's Law, and new life was breathed into the movement to have it heard and passed by the government.

The process was a complicated one. The founder of the Bill, Dan Sandor, immediately began urging citizens to sign petitions, and even more importantly, to write letters to the Prime Minister and the Minister of Justice, demonstrating a desire and a need for change.

At the direct political level, Councilor Gloria Lindsay Lub presented a petition to Toronto City Council at the end of March, 2006, with over fifteen hundred signatures, and moved to have the City of Toronto officially urge the Government of Canada to make intentional harm of a law enforcement animal an indictable offense.

Many police boards supported this movement and the Canadian Association of Police Boards drew up an official resolution to show their support of the new law.

The Bill had been continually reintroduced to Parliament since it's creation in 1999, but had run into trouble over and over. Members of Parliament widely supported the Bill, which had survived countless hours of hearings and debates, but it had been either blocked by Senate or dissolved because of elections and changes in government. Every time a new party took over the government, all Bills were dissolved and needed to be reintroduced.

It was reintroduced as Brigadier's Law for a first reading in Parliament on October, 2006. Changing a law is a very long, slow process, often taking several years to accomplish. Those who loved Brigadier, and who love all animals, know it is worth fighting for. This fight goes on.

On January 15, 2007, Dirk Sankersingh received a two-year conditional sentence for dangerous operation of a motor vehicle causing bodily harm and failure to stop at the scene of an accident causing bodily harm – a mere slap on the wrist, as most agreed.

Support for Brigadier's Law, and honoring the memory of this beautiful animal, continued across the country in the year following his death.

In April 2006, the Humane Society of Canada presented a posthumous Animal Heroes Award to Brigadier. This was graciously accepted by Kevin Bradfield, who was experiencing great physical and emotional difficulties, still healing from his own wounds and having a hard time coming to terms with the incident and the death of his partner.

The University of Guelph Veterinary Hospital set up the Brigadier Memorial Fund in memory of the special gelding. A beautiful poster was designed and made available to the public for twenty-five dollars. The proceeds from its sale, as well as donations made by citizens, have raised over thirty-seven thousand dollars to date.

The money is used to support clinical care for horses at the Large Animal Clinic.

On July 7, 2006, a plaque honoring Brigadier, was unveiled during a fundraiser at the Spirit of the Horse Memorial Garden in Langley, BC.

The Northumberland Humane Society began the Annual Brig's Walk, to encourage support of Brigadier's Law and keep the public focused on the need to change the laws for the benefit of all animals. This has become a much-anticipated spring event.

And, at the Police Equestrian Championships, where Brigadier "showed 'em all how to do it," the high point achievers in the Equitation and Obstacle Course classes are now awarded the Brigadier Memorial Champion Award.

All of this for a horse who did little more than lower his head to the level of children, make grown men laugh, and carry his partners for endless hours in all kinds of weather, in order to do his job. There is no question that he earned and deserved every bit of recognition!

Brigadier's stall stood empty and silent for months after his death, with only his gleaming halter on the door to remind people of the horse that had once occupied that space. In time, even this would change.

Nine months after Brigadier's death, David Carson

donated another golden chestnut Belgian cross three-year-old gelding to the unit, to "show a little support." The gelding was a sweet-natured horse who loved to nuzzle and rub on people, and whose initial training looked promising. The officers of the Mounted Unit were delighted, although they knew no horse could ever replace their Brigadier. A newcomer was always welcome, though, and this horse had a special place to fill. He was received enthusiastically.

It was decided that this horse should be named by the public, as a way to let people feel in touch and continue to heal from the loss of Brig. A "Name-The-Horse-Contest" was announced, and over eighteen hundred entries were received. In the end, it was a name suggested by Virginia O'Hearn that caught everyone's attention. She had suggested Commodore, which is the naval equivalent rank to an army Brigadier. It was a perfect fit, and the newcomer was officially welcomed to the Mounted Unit and given his name on Saturday, November 4, 2006 at the Royal Agricultural Winter Fair at Ricoh Coliseum.

Time passed and things changed within the Mounted Unit. Ted Gallipeau retired and moved away from the Toronto area. Ron Gilbert was moved into the Quarter

Masters post and he, in turn, offered Blue Moon to Vicki Montgomery as a permanent partner. Tim Crone was assigned to the Mounted Unit several months after Brig's death, a move he is very grateful for. Nothing that he had experienced in the ETF had ever affected him as badly as that night with Brigadier, and time spent with the Mounted Unit was like a healing salve on a burned soul.

Kevin Bradfield returned to work several months later, still suffering from back pain and sadness, but needing to get back into the stable and into his work in order to move forward.

Now, two years later, Kevin has a new partner named Charger, whom he still calls Brig now and then by mistake. Charger is an outstanding police horse in his own right, but for Kevin, none will ever replace Brigadier. The long days in the saddle and the physical work in the stable continue to plague the young man. After mucking stalls and lugging hay bales and buckets, his back is often sore before he even starts his six-hour patrol and he sometimes has to ride sidesaddle on the way home to endure the pain.

Kevin still loves the Mounted Unit and wants to be there more than anywhere else. He enjoys the camaraderie around the stable, the horses, the people, and he takes pride in his work. The pain in his back threatens his time there, though, and the pain in his heart has been slow to heal, too. His one wish is to be able to have one more battle of wills on the way home with Brigadier, to endure the bouncing and pulling of the "homing" gelding. The only difference, he says, is that this time, he'd let Brig win.

Brigadier's ashes and the display of the gifts sent after his death remained in the front lobby of the Horse Palace for two years. On January 10, 2008, exactly seven years to the day of his arrival at the unit, Brigadier's ashes were sent to the Thistledown Pet Memorial in Uxbridge, not far from Ron Gilbert's home, where he will rest in peace forever more.

Death touches all of us eventually – sometimes peacefully, sometimes violently, sometimes early, and sometimes after many long years of life. Brigadier, the gentle hero, had a short life with a violent end, but every day of his time on earth was a gift to every person who knew him. He touched hearts, brought smiles, and eased the pain of being human. He loved innocently and unconditionally.

That love and that special horse will never be forgotten.